# Princess Power

By Andrea Mills

**Senior Editor** Satu Hämeenaho-Fox
**Project Editor** Kritika Gupta
**Editorial Assistant** Abi Luscombe
**US Senior Editor** Shannon Beatty
**Project Art Editors** Emma Hobson, Roohi Rais
**Assistant Art Editors** Simran Lakhiani, Shubhi Srivastava
**Jacket Coordinator** Issy Walsh
**Jacket Designer** Emma Hobson
**DTP Designers** Vijay Kandwal, Sachin Gupta
**Project Picture Researcher** Aditya Katyal
**Producer, Pre-Production** Dragana Puvacic
**Senior Producer** Ena Matagic
**Managing Editors** Laura Gilbert, Monica Saigal
**Managing Art Editor** Diane Peyton Jones
**Deputy Managing Art Editor** Ivy Sengupta
**Delhi Team Head** Malavika Talukder
**Creative Director** Helen Senior
**Publishing Director** Sarah Larter

**Reading Consultant** Dr. Linda Gambrell
**Subject Consultant** Dr. Elena Woodacre

First American Edition, 2019
Published in the United States by DK Publishing
1450 Broadway, Suite 801, New York, NY 10018

A catalog record for this book
is available from the Library of Congress.
ISBN: 978-1-4654-8545-8 (Paperback)
ISBN: 978-1-4654-8547-2 (Hardcover)

DK books are available at special discounts when purchased in bulk for sales promotions,
premiums, fund-raising, or educational use. For details, contact: DK Publishing Special Markets,
1450 Broadway, Suite 801, New York, NY 10018
SpecialSales@dk.com

Printed and bound in China

The publisher would like to thank the following for their kind permission to reproduce their photographs:
(Key: a-above; b-below/bottom; c-center; f-far; l-left; r-right; t-top)
**3 Getty Images**: Fine Art / Corbis Historical. **4–5 Alamy Stock Photo**: ZUMA Press, Inc.. **10–11 Getty Images**: Universal History Archive / UIG.
**12–13 Alamy Stock Photo**: Classic Image. **14–15 Getty Images**: Camille Silvy / Stringer / Hulton Royals Collection. **17 Alamy Stock Photo**:
Moviestore collection Ltd. **18 Alamy Stock Photo**: Antiques & Collectables (clb, crb). **19 Alamy Stock Photo**: Heritage Image Partnership Ltd (clb,
cb); The History Collection (cla); World History Archive (cr). **Getty Images**: Heritage Images / Hulton Fine Art Collection (c); PHAS / UIG (ca). **21
Alamy Stock Photo**: The History Collection. **22 Alamy Stock Photo**: Anil Dave. **25 Alamy Stock Photo**: Historic Collection. **26 Alamy Stock Photo**:
The Granger Collection. **28 Alamy Stock Photo**: Heritage Image Partnership Ltd. **29 Alamy Stock Photo**: Dinodia Photos (crb). **Getty Images**:
Apic / Hulton Archive (cra). **30 Alamy Stock Photo**: Hi-Story. **31 Getty Images**: Print Collector / Hulton Archive. **32 Getty Images**: Anwar Hussein
/ WireImage. **33 Getty Images**: Tim Graham / Tim Graham Photo Library. **35 Alamy Stock Photo**: The Picture Art Collection. **36–37 Alamy Stock
Photo**: Dinodia Photos. **38 Alamy Stock Photo**: Lebrecht Music & Arts (clb). **Dreamstime.com**: Etraveler (clb/Old Paper). **38–39 Alamy Stock
Photo**: INTERFOTO / History (c). **Dreamstime.com**: Thitisaichua (c/Photo frame). **39 123RF.com**: Ozgur Guvenc (br); mahirates (cb); photomelon
(cr). **41 Getty Images**: Fine Art / Corbis Historical. **42–43 Alamy Stock Photo**: History and Art Collection. **45 Alamy Stock Photo**: Classic Image.
**46–47 Alamy Stock Photo**: The Print Collector. **48 Getty Images**: Max Mumby / Indigo. **49 Getty Images**: Keystone / Stringer / Hulton Royals
Collection (cla); Pascal Le Segretain (cr); Michel Porro / WireImage (clb). **50 Getty Images**: Michelly Rall / WireImage. **51 Getty Images**: Andreas
Rentz. **52–53 Getty Images**: The Asahi Shimbun. **54 Dreamstime.com**: Maciej Gillert. **55 Alamy Stock Photo**: newsphoto. **57 Getty Images**: WPA
Pool / Pool. **63 Alamy Stock Photo**: Heritage Image Partnership Ltd

**Cover images:** *Front:* **Dreamstime.com**: Natee Srisuk (Background); **Getty Images**: Anwar Hussein;
*Back:* **Alamy Stock Photo**: Interfoto / Personalities t

All other images © Dorling Kindersley
For further information see: www.dkimages.com

# A WORLD OF IDEAS:
## SEE ALL THERE IS TO KNOW

**www.dk.com**

# Contents

# Chapter 1
# An introduction to princesses

Classic stories and fairy-tale films show pretty princesses waiting for their prince to save them. However, history tells us that princesses do much more than this. Princesses are important members of royal families. Most are the daughter or granddaughter of a reigning king or queen. Ordinary women can also become princesses by marrying a prince. In the past, princesses were not always very powerful, but many of them showed incredible bravery in difficult times.

Today, many princesses work hard to help others, and support charities and causes they feel passionate about.

Princess Madeleine of Sweden at the wedding of her sister Princess Victoria in June 2010.

# Royal family tree

Every royal family has a line of succession. This is the order in which members become king or queen. In the past, the oldest son was normally the successor, but in many countries today girls have equal opportunities to reign. This is an example of a European royal family tree.

## Siblings of reigning monarch

The brothers and sisters of the reigning monarch can often inherit the crown if the sovereign has no children.

**Key**

............... Siblings

————— Children

 Marriage

In line for the throne

## Sovereign

A sovereign is the reigning queen, king, chief, or leader of a country.

## Husband or wife of reigning monarch

The partner of the monarch is called their consort.

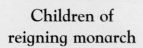

## Children of reigning monarch

Children of the reigning monarch are given titles such as prince/princess or duke/duchess.

## Husband or wife of princes and princesses

The husband or wife of the monarch's children are usually given similar titles to their partner. So, often a prince's wife would be a princess and a duke's wife would be a duchess.

## Grandchildren of reigning monarch

The monarch's grandchildren are also in the line of succession.

Pingyang was born into a noble family. She used her strength and determination to become a mighty princess in China. In the 7th century, she refused to listen to Emperor Yangdi of China. She formed an army called "the Army of the Lady." The Emperor did not take the army seriously because it was led by a woman, until Pingyang had gathered 70,000 soldiers.

Princess Pingyang was buried with the honors of a soldier, which was rare for any woman of that time.

Pingyang led her army
into battle against the
unpopular ruling Sui
dynasty, and won.
When her father,
a nobleman, became
the first emperor of the
new Tang dynasty,
Pingyang was made
a princess.

Indigenous American Pocahontas was a peacekeeper between different local people, such as the Powhatan, and English settlers in the 17th century. When the English moved closer to the Powhatan people's homes, trouble arose. However, Pocahontas showed generosity and kindness to both sides.

Her father, Chief Powhatan, captured the English leader. Pocahontas begged him to show forgiveness. Legend claims that she gave food to the settlers and fought for the release of Powhatan prisoners.

Pocahontas married an English settler and together they helped keep the peace. The couple eventually moved to England, where Pocahontas met King James I.

A painting of Pocahontas at the court of King James I of England by the American artist Richard Rummels.

Anne Neville played an important part in the series of English wars known as the Wars of the Roses (1455–1487). Anne's father, the Earl of Warwick, arranged her marriage to Edward, the son of Henry VI, as an agreement to end the war. This made Anne the Princess of Wales. Unfortunately, her father and husband died in battle.

Later, Anne married King Richard III to become the new queen of England. She ruled for two years until she died. In 1960, a bronze plaque was placed at her tomb in Westminster Abbey in London, to make sure she is remembered.

Anne Neville features as a character in the play *Richard III* by William Shakespeare.

Aina was born a princess in the Yoruba dynasty of West Africa in 1843. When her parents died, she was kidnapped and enslaved. In 1850, she met British captain Frederick Forbes, who was in West Africa to work against slavery. He arranged for Aina to travel to England. He also gave her the new name Sarah Forbes Bonetta.

When she arrived in England, the young girl was presented to Queen Victoria. The queen liked Sarah and paid for her education. Later, Sarah named her daughter Victoria after the monarch who changed her life.

Sarah Forbes Bonetta with her husband, James Davies, in September 1862.

American actress Grace Kelly was a movie star of the 20th century. Starting out in television dramas, she soon moved on to Hollywood films. Success on the big screen resulted in fame as well as an Oscar™ for her role in *The Country Girl* in 1955. However, she would become more famous when she married Prince Rainier of Monaco the following year.

The princess created a new life with her three children and involvement in charity work. Sadly, in 1982 she died in a car crash. Grace Kelly's films are still watched by many people today.

Grace Kelly with her husband, Prince Rainier III, on their wedding day in April 1956.

# Happy endings?

In the past, royal marriages were arranged. Sometimes the pair didn't know each other before they got married and they didn't always like each other either.

Married: 1152–1189

**Eleanor of Aquitaine**
Ambitious Eleanor was a queen two times, first marrying the king of France and later the king of England (shown above).

## Catherine of Aragon

This princess and later queen was the first wife of King Henry VIII. They were married for 24 years until a historic divorce brought it to an end.

Married: 1509–1533

## Sophia Dorothea

German princess Sophia Dorothea had an arranged marriage with her cousin King George I. He imprisoned her for more than 30 years.

Married: 1682–1694

## Marie Antoinette

Marie Antoinette became queen of France when her husband, Louis, was crowned king. During the French Revolution, they were both executed.

Married: 1770–1793

# Chapter 2
# Rebel princesses

Known as the "She-wolf of France," Princess Isabella was a strong-minded woman. She was the only surviving daughter of King Philip IV of France. Isabella married King Edward II of England in 1308 and became a queen. However, they did not always get along. Isabella was angry when Edward favored his friends over her and took her land. So, she took revenge. She helped the french invade England, which caused King Edward II to be taken off the throne. He was replaced by their son Edward III in 1327.

Isabella ruled as regent for three years and later joined a convent living alongside nuns.

When she invaded England, Isabella captured the Tower of London.

Princess Mira Bai (1498–1546) rejected the traditional behavior expected of a princess in India. Instead, Mira spent her life worshipping the Hindu god Krishna. These unusual ways brought disapproval from her family. However, she remained faithful to her god. She used her creativity and commitment to write about 1,300 poems, known as *bhajans*, for Krishna. Although born into riches, Mira chose to live among the poor. Her poems are still sung in India today, where she is considered a saint.

A stained glass window of Mira Bai playing the *ektara*, a single-stringed musical instrument, for the god Krishna.

Princess Sophia Duleep Singh (1876–1948) was a leading figure of the suffragette movement in the UK. The Suffragettes fought for equal rights for women. Sophia was the daughter of the last Maharaja (Indian prince) of the Sikh Empire (now part of India). Sophia grew up surrounded by riches. However, the princess spent her life fighting for women's rights.

Sophia played an important part in suffragette campaigns. She protested alongside famous women's campaigner Emmeline Pankhurst. When Pankhurst died in 1928, Sophia became President of the Suffragette Fellowship. She also joined the Women's Tax Resistance League. She believed that women should not pay taxes if they could not vote.

Princess Sophia selling *The Suffragette* newspaper in the UK in 1913.

Queen Liliuokalani wrote more than 150 songs.

Queen Liliuokalani was the only queen of Hawaii and the country's last ruling monarch. Liliuokalani was a talented musician and songwriter, who wrote the well-known song "Aloha 'Oe." In 1874, her family was elected as the next royal bloodline, as there was no heir to the Hawaiian king.

Princess Liliuokalani replaced her brother to become queen in 1891. As queen, Liliuokalani fought to protect the independence of the Hawaiian islands. America decided to invade Hawaii to regain power. Liliuokalani was forced to give up after a two-year reign. Hawaii became a republic in 1894 and an official US state in 1959.

# Princess warriors

In the past, royal women have shown bravery in battle and used clever tactics to win wars.

Urraca of Zamora

Urraca of Zamora (1033–1101), daughter of the king of León (now a part of Spain), went into battle against her brother after he attacked her kingdom. She won and her brother was killed.

## Khutulun

Mongol princess Khutulun (1260–1306) was a celebrated warrior and wrestler who never lost a fight.

## Amina of Zazzau

African princess Amina (1533–1610) trained to be a warrior. As ruler of Zazzau (now a part of Nigeria), she used her skills to expand her kingdom's land.

## Manikarnika Tambe

A princess by marriage, Manikarnika Tambe (1828–1858) died while fighting the British in the struggle for Indian independence in 1858.

# Chapter 3
# Caring princesses

Princess Alice proved she had a heart of gold as a lifelong caregiver. The third child of Queen Victoria and Prince Albert, she was born in Buckingham Palace in 1843. Growing up, she took care of her six younger siblings and visited injured soldiers from the Crimean War (1853–1856) in the hospital. This sparked an interest in healthcare.

Princess Alice

Alice cared for her grandmother until she died in 1861. She also took care of her father. During the Austro-Prussian War (1866), she was in charge of field hospitals, which were set up for the injured. Alice caught the disease diphtheria and died in 1878.

Princess Alice with her father, Prince Albert.

Princess Diana is one of the most famous women in recent history because of her caring nature. Diana Spencer became very popular when she began dating Prince Charles, the son of Queen Elizabeth II. The couple married in 1981 and had two sons, William and Harry. However, the marriage did not last.

After the divorce, people still loved Diana. She helped many charities and supported groups that cared for the sick and elderly.

Princess Diana on a trip to New Zealand in April 1983.

Princess Diana walking through a minefield that was cleared by a charity called HALO in Huambo, Angola.

Her campaign to stop the use of dangerous landmines led to a global ban. Diana died in a car accident in 1997 and 2.5 billion people watched her funeral worldwide.

This medieval princess turned her back on riches to help the poor and needy. Agnes, daughter of King Ottokar I and Queen Constance of Bohemia, was born in 1211 in what is now the Czech Republic. She received several marriage proposals from European kings. But instead, Agnes chose to devote herself to her religion. She cared for others, and helped build hospitals and monasteries. Although Agnes was born a princess, she preferred to care for the sick than to live a life of luxury. Agnes died in 1282 and more than 700 years later was made a saint.

Painting of Agnes of Bohemia taking care of a sick person in 1482.

Princess Gayatri Devi showed lots of care and kindness in her life. She was born in 1919, the daughter of a Maharaja. In 1940, Gayatri married the Maharaja of Jaipur. She fought for women's rights and established the Gayatri Devi School in 1943. This turned into one of the best girls' schools in India.

Princess Gayatri Devi speaking with villagers in Jaipur, India, during her election campaign in 1962.

In 1962, Gayatri became the first woman to win a seat in the Indian Parliament. She died in 2009 and remains an inspiration for women in politics.

# Mythical princesses

Once upon a time, traditional stories were written about princesses who triumphed over evil and lived happily ever after.

**Cinderella**
In this 1697 French fairy tale, a pumpkin is magically turned into a carriage, with mice as horses, so that Cinderella can go to the royal ball.

## Snow White

The Brothers Grimm wrote *Snow White* in 1812 in Germany. A girl falls asleep after eating a poisoned apple. She can only be saved by a kiss from her true love.

## Princess Badroulbadour

Aladdin was part of the book *Arabian Nights*. Princess Badroulbadour wins Aladdin's heart, and a magic lamp brings them good and bad fortunes.

## The Little Mermaid

In 1837, Danish author Hans Christian Andersen published *The Little Mermaid*. A mermaid takes a witch's potion to grow human legs.

# Chapter 4
# Princesses
# to queens

Queen Elizabeth I ruled over a "golden age" in England, known for peace, power, and success. Born in 1553, Elizabeth was the daughter of King Henry VIII and Anne Boleyn. Princess Elizabeth's childhood was difficult. Henry had her mother executed. He later married again another four times. When her half sister, Queen Mary, died in 1558, Elizabeth replaced her on the throne for the next 44 years.

England grew under her rule. Trade (buying and selling) between different countries boomed, and the arts developed. Elizabeth died in 1603 and is remembered as one of the finest leaders in history.

A painting of Princess Elizabeth I at age 13 by Tudor artist, William Scrots.

A portrait of Princess Victoria at age 14 with her spaniel, Dash.

Princess Victoria was born in 1819, and grew up in royal luxury. She had a private tutor, who taught her lessons in many languages. The princess was fifth in line to the throne and was not expected to ever become monarch. Her cousin Charlotte, Princess of Wales, was meant to be queen instead of Victoria, but Charlotte died when she was 21.

In 1837, Victoria became queen at the age of 18 when her uncle William IV died. She fell in love with a German prince named Albert. They married and had nine children including Princess Alice. Victoria reigned for 63 years.

The United Kingdom's Queen Elizabeth II is the great-great-granddaughter of Queen Victoria. Born in 1926, Princess Elizabeth Windsor was the oldest daughter of the Duke and Duchess of York. Elizabeth and her little sister, Margaret, were educated at home by a governess. The young princess loved animals, particularly dogs and horses. When her father was crowned king in 1936, Elizabeth became the next in line to the throne.

As a young woman in World War II, she trained as a driver and mechanic in the British Army. However, she was destined to become queen.

A childhood picture of Queen Elizabeth II (*left*) with her sister, Princess Margaret (*right*).

Princess Elizabeth found out about her father's death while on vacation in 1952. She became queen immediately. Her coronation was held in Westminster Abbey on June 2, 1953. At her side was her husband, Prince Philip, Duke of Edinburgh. It was the first British coronation to be shown on television. Celebrations took place all over the world.

Queen Elizabeth II (*far right*) on her coronation day with her maids of honor.

In 2017, Queen Elizabeth II became the first British monarch to celebrate a Sapphire Jubilee. This marked an incredible 65 years on the throne. She is very popular and crowds often line the streets to see her.

# Royal sisterhood

Princess sisters are at the heart of many royal families around the world, with some destined to be future queens.

**Eugenie and Beatrice**
Beatrice and Eugenie are daughters of the British Duke and Duchess of York. Beatrice (*right*) works for a technology company, while Eugenie (*left*) is director of an art gallery.

### Sirindhorn, Chulabhorn, and Ubolratana

These sisters from Thailand are also siblings of King Maha Vajiralongkorn. Princess Ubolratana (*far right*) started a charity in Thailand to support young people.

### Caroline and Stéphanie

The Prince of Monaco and Grace Kelly had two daughters. Caroline (*left*) is a patron of the arts and Stéphanie (*right*) is involved in a lot of charity work.

### Ariane, Catharina-Amalia, and Alexia

As eldest daughter of King Willem-Alexander and Queen Maxima of the Netherlands, Princess Catharina-Amalia (*middle*) will one day be queen.

# Chapter 5
# Modern princesses

Before she became a princess, Charlene Wittstock was already attracting attention. She was born in 1978 in Zimbabwe. Her family moved to South Africa when she was 12. There, she developed a love of swimming that took her to the Olympics. Charlene competed for South Africa at the Sydney Games in 2000.

Princess Charlene

Princess Charlene and Prince Albert II
on their wedding day in 2011.

She then won three gold medals at the
swimming World Cup two years later.
Charlene met Prince Albert of Monaco
at a swimming competition. They married
in 2011, making Charlene the Princess
of Monaco. She has since given birth to
twins and shows support for many charities.

Crown Princess Masako after her wedding ceremony at the Tokyo Imperial Palace in 1993.

When a young Japanese diplomat (person who represents their country in another country) fell in love with a crown prince, her life was changed forever. Owada Masako was born in 1963. She studied at both Harvard and Oxford universities. Masako became a junior diplomat, like her father. She could speak many languages, which made her a talented translator.

Masako met the Crown Prince Naruhito at a tea party in 1986. Later, they married, making Masako the Crown Princess of Japan. In 2019, Emperor Akihito abdicated (stepped down). This made Masako the new Empress of Japan.

Prince William and the Duchess of Cambridge during a Royal Tour of Germany and Poland in July 2017.

This story of an ordinary girl marrying the future king of the United Kingdom is a modern-day fairy tale. Born in 1982, Kate had a happy childhood and an excellent education. At the University of St. Andrews, she met Queen Elizabeth II's grandson Prince William. Friendship blossomed into love.

The two married in 2011 at Westminster Abbey. Two billion people worldwide watched as Kate was crowned Her Royal Highness, the Duchess of Cambridge. She remains hugely popular and draws crowds wherever she goes. The couple have three children. Princess Charlotte, their daughter, was born in 2015 and is the fourth in line to the throne.

Duchess of Cambridge, Catherine, with her daughter Princess Charlotte.

The young Meghan Markle had no idea that she would one day marry into a royal family. Meghan was born in 1981 and grew up in California. She became a television and film actress.

Meghan met Prince Harry in 2016 and the pair quickly fell in love. They married at Windsor Castle in 2018. Meghan became Her Royal Highness, the Duchess of Sussex. Meghan has also worked with the United Nations, an organization set up to keep the peace between countries. She has helped them fight for equality for women. In 2019, the Duke and Duchess of Sussex had their first child, Archie.

Prince Harry and the Duchess of Sussex, Meghan Markle, on their wedding day in May 2018.

# Quiz

**1** What was Princess Pingyang's army called?

**2** What did Sarah Forbes Bonetta name her daughter?

**3** Which princess was known as the "She-wolf of France"?

**4** Which god did Mira Bai honor in her poems?

**5** During which war did Princess Alice manage field hospitals for the injured?

**6** Which princess was the first woman to win a seat in the Indian Parliament?

**7** Which princess's mother was executed by King Henry VIII?

**8** How old was Princess Victoria when she became queen?

**9** What year was Elizabeth II crowned?

**10** Which princess and later queen wrote the song "Aloha 'Oe"?

**11** Where did the Duchess of Cambridge meet Prince William?

**12** What title was Meghan Markle given when she married Prince Harry?

Answers on page 61

# Glossary

**bloodline**
person's relatives and ancestors

**campaign**
carrying out a set of actions to achieve a goal

**coronation**
ceremony where someone is officially crowned
king or queen

**empire**
group of countries ruled over by another country
or monarch

**equality**
the same rights for everyone

**execution**
when a person is sentenced to death

**heir**
person who is next in line to the throne

**indigenous people**
people who lived in an area before any
settlers arrived

**invasion**
entering another country without permission
and trying to claim it as one's own

**monarch**
king or queen of a country

**noble**
important person in society who often owns a lot of land

**protest**
to disagree with something and fight for change

**regent**
person who rules a country when the monarch is unable to, often because they are too young

**republic**
countries that are not ruled by monarchs

**succession**
order in which members of the royal family become king or queen

**suffragettes**
group of women who fought for women's right to vote

**tax**
money that every working person pays to the government

**Answers to the quiz:**
1. The Army of the Lady; 2. Victoria; 3. Princess Isabella;
4. Krishna; 5. Austro-Prussian War; 6. Gayatri Devi; 7. Queen
Elizabeth I; 8. 18 years old; 9. 1953; 10. Liliuokalani;
11. University of St. Andrews; 12. Duchess of Sussex

# Index

Urraca of Zamora

# A LEVEL FOR EVERY READER

This book is a part of an exciting four-level reading series to support children in developing the habit of reading widely for both pleasure and information. Each book is designed to develop a child's reading skills, fluency, grammar awareness, and comprehension in order to build confidence and enjoyment when reading.

## Ready for a Level 3 (Beginning to Read Alone) book

A child should:

- be able to read many words without needing to stop and break them down into sound parts.
- read smoothly, in phrases and with expression, and at a good pace.
- self-correct when a word or sentence doesn't sound right or doesn't make sense.

## A valuable and shared reading experience

For many children, reading requires much effort but adult participation can make reading both fun and easier. Here are a few tips on how to use this book with a young reader:

*Check out the contents together:*

- read about the book on the back cover and talk about the contents page to help heighten interest and expectation.
- ask the reader to make predictions about what they think will happen next.
- talk about the information he/she might want to find out.

*Encourage fluent reading:*

- encourage reading aloud in fluent, expressive phrases, making full use of punctuation, and thinking about the meaning; if helpful, choose a sentence to read aloud to help demonstrate reading with expression.

*Praise, share, and talk:*

- notice if the reader is responding to the text by self-correcting and varying his/her voice.
- encourage the reader to recall specific details after each chapter.
- let her/him pick out interesting words and discuss what they mean.
- talk about what he/she found most interesting or important and show your own enthusiasm for the book.
- read the quiz at the end of the book and encourage the reader to answer the questions, if necessary, by turning back to the relevant pages to find the answers.

Series consultant, Dr. Linda Gambrell, Emerita Distinguished Professor of Education at Clemson University, has served as President of the National Reading Conference, the College Reading Association, and the International Reading Association.